Strange But True
Basketball Stories

Strange But True Basketball Stories

by

HOWARD LISS

illustrated with photographs

RANDOM HOUSE NEW YORK

For Bob and Mike Shlan—
a couple of great basketball fans

Library of Congress Cataloging in Publication Data:
Liss, Howard. Strange but true basketball stories.
(The Random House sports library)
SUMMARY: Eighteen true stories of unique events in basketball include accounts
of the Rio Grande College team, the Harlem Globetrotters, Wilt Chamberlain,
and other high scorers and fancy shooters.
1. Basketball—Addresses, essays, lectures—Juvenile literature.
[1. Basketball]   I. Title.   II. Series.   GV885.1.L52   1983   796.32'32   82-13138
ISBN: 0-394-85631-7 (pbk.)

Manufactured in the United States of America
1   2   3   4   5   6   7   8   9   0

Contents

Introduction

Basketball is the newest of the team sports. Baseball, football, hockey, soccer, and lacrosse were all being played when basketball was invented in the fall of 1891. But basketball need not take a back seat to other sports as far as strange stories are concerned. In fact, more peculiar things have happened during basketball games than in any other sport. One reason may be that it is played throughout the world. Soccer and basketball are the world's most popular games. One old magazine reports that in 1931 a three-night basketball tournament in Peking, China, drew a total of 72,000 paying fans!

Basketball is played on a comparatively small court, yet the players cover a great deal of ground in a game. About twenty years ago a mathematician figured out how much territory the players crossed in a regulation college game. He found out that forwards travel five and one-half miles, centers run four miles, and guards move about three miles. And that's all done in just 40 minutes of playing time.

Officials and referees in all sports take plenty of abuse, and basketball is no exception. Yet it seems that crazier things happen to referees in basketball than in any other game. One time Artie Gore, a baseball umpire, was asked to officiate at a basketball game. Since he was familiar with all the rules of basketball, Gore agreed. It was a close game, and referee Gore called a number of fouls. After one foul he suddenly heard the player's coach shout from the bench, "Get that dirty dog out of here and don't let me see his face again!"

Gore was angry because he thought the coach was talking about him. He was ready to charge the coach with a technical foul when he saw him pointing across the court. Gore turned—and began to laugh. There actually was a mongrel dog, loping along the end lines.

The team with the greatest winning percentage in sports history was, of course, a basketball team. During the 1920s and 1930s the fabulous Original Celtics barnstormed throughout America. They won almost all the time, no matter where they went or whom they played. Over the years new players came to the team, but still the Celtics kept winning. By the time the team was disbanded in 1941, the Original Celtics had won 1,320 games and lost only 66!

Women have also been responsible for some basketball oddities. In 1950 a 15-year-old North Carolina girl named Aileen Cudd achieved a moment of great glory. Playing for the Green Creek High School team, she scored 95 points in a single game against Sunnyview High!

—Howard Liss

Strange But True
Basketball Stories

1·The New Game— Basketball

It was early autumn 1891. The baseball season was over and football was still a couple of weeks away. In New England it was already too cold for track and field (indoor running tracks did not exist at the time). And most young men didn't care for calisthenics or the traditional gym activities such as rope climbing. Organized athletics had come to a temporary standstill.

Dr. Luther Gulick, head of the International Young Men's Christian Association Training School, decided that a new kind of group exercise was needed to keep the students in good condition. He spoke to the faculty about it, asking them to think of a "team" activity.

One of the instructors at the school was a young man named James Naismith. He dimly remembered a game called "Duck on a Rock" that he had played with his friends

in his native Canada. Naismith thought that with some changes, the old game might be the answer to Dr. Gulick's request. He began to invent new rules for the game, and finally he had enough to test it.

One morning he borrowed a ladder and nailed two peach baskets to the walls of the gym, one basket at each end. He got a soccer ball from the athletic trunk and announced to his class that they were about to try a new sport. Since there were 18 students in his class, he divided them into teams of nine each. And because he was using peach baskets, he called the game "basketball."

Naismith explained that the idea of the game was simply to toss the ball into the baskets, which were 10 feet off the floor. He explained a few other rules, but it's doubtful that many of the players understood them at first.

They played anyway and had a marvelous time. Naismith kept the ladder handy to retrieve the ball since the bottoms had not been cut out of the peach baskets. It wasn't used much, though, for the final score was 1–0.

Dr. James Naismith

Other students heard about the game and wanted to try it. Soon everybody in the school was practicing shots at the baskets. To keep order, Naismith wrote out the rules and published them in the school paper on January 15, 1892:

The ball is to be an ordinary Association (soccer) football.

1. The ball may be thrown in any direction with one or both hands.

2. The ball may be batted in any direction with one or both hands (never with the fist).

3. A player cannot run with the ball. The player must throw it from the spot on which he catches it. . . .

4. The ball must be held in or between the hands; the arms or body must not be used for holding it.

5. No shouldering, holding, pushing, tripping, or striking in any way the person of the opponent shall be allowed; the first infringement of this rule by any player shall count as a foul; the second shall disqualify him until the next goal is made . . . with no substitute allowed.

6. A foul is striking the ball with the fist, violation of Rules 3, 4, and such as described in Rule 5.

7. If either side makes three consecutive fouls, it shall count as a goal for the opponents. . . .

8. A goal shall be made when the ball is thrown or batted *from the grounds* into the basket and stays there, providing those defending the goal do not touch or disturb the goal. If the ball rests on the edge and the opponents move the

basket, it shall count as a goal.

9. When the ball goes out of bounds, it shall be thrown into the field of play by the first person touching it. In case of a dispute, the umpire shall throw it straight into the field. The thrower-in is allowed five seconds; if he holds it longer, it shall go to an opponent. If any side persists in delaying the game, the umpire shall call a foul on that side.

10. The umpire shall be the judge of the men and shall note the fouls and notify the referee when three consecutive fouls have been made. He shall have the power to disqualify men according to Rule 5.

11. The referee shall be the judge of the ball and shall decide when the ball is in play, in bounds, to which side it belongs, and shall keep time. He shall decide when a goal has been made and keep account of the goals with any other duties that are performed by a referee.

12. The time shall be two fifteen-minute halves, with five minutes' rest between.

13. The side making the most goals in that time shall be declared the winner. In case of a draw the game may, by agreement of the captains, be continued until another goal has been made.

The number comprising a team depends largely on the size of the floor space, but it may range from three to a side to forty. The fewer players down to three, the more scientific it may be; but the more players the more fun. The men may be arranged according to the idea of the captain, but it has been found that a Goal Keeper, two Guards, three Center Men, two Wings and a Home Man stationed in the above order may be best.

7

Naismith (in street clothes) poses with the first basketball team in 1891.

It shall be the duty of the Goal Keeper and the two Guards to prevent the opponents from scoring. The duty of the Wing Men and the Home Man is to put the ball into the opponent's goal, and the Center Men shall feed the ball forward to the man who has the best opportunity, thus making nine the best number for a team.

Few of Naismith's original rules remain. For example, the rule of three fouls in a row counting as a goal for the opponents was soon dropped. But someone who broke the rules still had to be punished. So the free throw was adopted in 1894. A couple of years later the keyhole, the spot where free throws were to be taken, was marked on the court.

The center jump was first used in 1893. On January 16, 1896, the first college game was played between the University of Iowa and the University of Chicago. Each team used five men, and for some unexplained reason that became the standard size of a basketball team.

If any single type of action identifies basketball, it is the dribble. Strangely enough, no one is really sure how or when it started. For a long time the dribble was simply part of the game, but neither the players nor the officials knew how to regulate it. At one time the rules prohibited a player from shooting after he had dribbled. Not until 1915 could a man pop the ball at the basket after he had dribbled.

All sports have nicknames. Football is often referred to as the gridiron game, and baseball is known as the diamond game. Basketball is the "cage game," so named by a sportswriter for the Trenton *Daily American*. One day he was watching a game and remarked, "These fellows play like monkeys. They should be put into a cage."

The manager of the Trenton team overheard him and soon after enclosed the Trenton court with chicken wire eight feet high. This cage not only kept the players inside, but it kept the ball from going out of bounds. Later, rope netting replaced the metal wire, and the game became a hilarious spectacle as players bounced off the ropes all over the court.

Many things have changed since James Naismith first drew up the rules of basketball. Even the school where the game was born has a new name. The International YMCA Training School is now Springfield College. But perhaps the greatest change is in the game's popularity.

More people *watch* soccer than any other sport. But more people *play* basketball than any other game in the world!

2 · One Hand Is Better Than Two

In the early days of basketball, players were taught to shoot with two hands. The style was considered a fundamental. The players shot with a kind of straight-arm motion, tossing the ball forward with a flip of the wrists. This was supposed to give better ball control.

Today most players shoot with one hand. The man who popularized the one-handed shot was a 6-foot-3 scoring demon named Hank Luisetti.

Like so many stars, Hank began to fool around with a basketball when he was only six years old. At that time he shot using two hands just like the other kids. It wasn't until he was a teenager at Galileo High School in San Francisco that he began to develop the one-hander.

Hank couldn't explain why he suddenly took one hand off the ball when shooting. It just happened one day, and it worked. Somehow the one-handed shot gave him exactly the right touch. His shot was incredibly accurate, and although it was unorthodox, his coach didn't want to tamper with a good thing. Of course Hank often used the two-handed shot too.

Hank went on to Stanford University, where he joined the basketball team. He asked coach Johnny Bunn if he could continue using his one-handed shot. "Let's see a sample," said Bunn. Hank shot from the corner and the ball swished in. "Stay with it, boy," Bunn smiled.

He did, leading the freshman team to an undefeated season. He scored 305 points in 18 games, averaging almost 17 points per game.

In the middle 1930s the best basketball teams were in the East, and the best team in the East was Long Island University. Coached by Clair Bee, the LIU team had won 43 games in a row. They were fast and rough, and they were excellent shooters.

On December 30, 1936, Stanford came to

Stanford's Hank Luisetti in 1938.

New York City to battle LIU. By this time Luisetti was quite famous. In fact, Stanford had beaten a strong Temple team just a few days earlier, and Luisetti had been the key figure in that victory. That year he had averaged 22 points per game—a very high figure in those days. Still, most of Stanford's wins had been against western clubs, and none of them were considered as good as LIU.

LIU scored first against Stanford and held the lead for the first few minutes. Stanford was having trouble mounting a counter-attack. Then Hank Luisetti, guarded closely by big Art Hillhouse, jumped and shot the ball one-handed—*swish!*

Hillhouse was amazed. He had never seen anyone try a shot like that, and for a few moments he thought it just a lucky toss. It wasn't. Stanford finally broke the game open and walked off with a 45–31 victory. Luisetti was high man with 15 points.

Stanford, and especially Hank Luisetti, received a great deal of praise after their victory. Clair Bee said flatly that Luisetti was the best player he had ever seen.

Despite Hank's great ability to score, he was reluctant to shoot. He enjoyed passing off to his teammates more than he liked to take a pop at the basket. In fact, the other Stanford players often had to beg Hank to take his share of shots.

Once, against Duquesne, Hank was busily feeding the ball to his teammates when they decided to force him into shooting. Luisetti passed the ball to his center, Art Stoefen, who promptly passed it back to Hank under the basket. But Hank threw back to Stoefen, and he scored. The next time Stanford got the ball, Luisetti found himself in a passing feud with teammate Howie Turner. Finally Luisetti got the message and dumped the ball in.

That game Hank Luisetti scored a whopping 50 points!

Even though Luisetti scored consistently with his one-handed shot, some coaches were still skeptical. Nat Holman, who had been a great player in his day, said, "I'll quit coaching if I have to teach one-handed shots to win." But even Holman had to admit that Luisetti was a spectacular passer and dribbler.

Still, Holman could do or say little about the changes that followed. In a short time kids all over the country were flipping the ball up with one hand, imitating Luisetti's technique.

Basketball has undergone a great many changes over the years, but few compare to the one-handed shot "invented" by Hank Luisetti.

3 · The Story of an Olympic Star

Hank Iba, the basketball coach at Oklahoma State, had been chosen to coach the U.S. Olympic basketball team in the 1968 Olympic Games. Tryouts for the team were fast approaching, and Iba thought that his squad might well be the finest group of players in basketball history. He was counting on such college superstars as Lew Alcindor (now Kareem Abdul-Jabbar), Elvin Hayes, Wes Unseld, Bob Lanier, Don May, Mike Lewis, and others to make the team. That group had speed, height, shooting ability, and aggressiveness. The 7-foot-2 Alcindor could make the difference all by himself, for the Russians had a strong club and a 7-foot-3 pivot man.

But 1968 was not an ordinary year. Many athletes, both black and white, were angry at the mistreatment of minority groups. America was torn by civil disorder. There were bitter, sometimes violent demonstrations on college campuses. A number of athletes of all races and religions decided to protest in the most forceful way they could. They would not come out for the Olympics. One particular reason for the Olympic boycott was the participation in the games of the Union of South Africa, where athletes of different colors could not compete together.

Hank Iba was left without Alcindor, Hayes, Unseld, Lanier, and May. He conducted the tryouts anyway and made his selections. American Olympic officials shook their heads sadly at what they thought was a weak team. The U.S. Olympic team would be lucky to make the basketball quarterfinals. The team was expected to lose to the Russians and would probably lose to Yugoslavia as well.

None of the players selected by Iba had the reputations of Alcindor, Hayes, Unseld, May, or Lanier. But as they continued to practice, they welded themselves into a hard-driving unit. It became evident that this wasn't such a bad team after all.

The team leader was Jo Jo White, a 6-foot-3 guard from Kansas. White had fast hands, and he could pass, fake, set up plays, and shoot. Others were Calvin Fowler of Akron, Bill Hoskett of Ohio State, Ken Spain of Houston, Glynn Solters of Northeast Louisiana, and Charlie Scott of North Carolina. There was also a 6-foot-8, 19-year-old eager beaver from Detroit named Spencer Haywood. Hank Iba's eyes popped when he saw Haywood perform. Later he said that Haywood would have made the team even if all the superstars he wanted had shown up for the tryouts.

In a way it was strange that Haywood was not one of those boycotting the Olympics. The protesters had refused to come because they wanted to dramatize the plight of underprivileged blacks all over the world. And yet few had had a more deprived childhood than young Spencer Haywood.

He was born and brought up in Silver City, Mississippi, on the banks of the sluggish Yazoo River. Spencer's father died of overwork, the result of laboring 14 hours a day as a carpenter. His mother scrubbed floors, and welfare gave the family an additional $10 a month. But that wasn't enough to buy shoes and clothing for the 10 children in the family.

So all the Haywood kids worked. Spencer

earned four dollars a day by picking 200 pounds of cotton, working from dawn till sundown. In the summer the temperature rose to 110 degrees, but the child kept picking cotton because his family needed the money.

But it wasn't the work Spencer minded so much, nor was it sleeping three in a bed with his brothers. It was the gnawing hunger pains in his stomach—the family ate only one meal a day. It was the slaps and the insults; it was being called "nigger" by cruel, unthinking whites.

Spencer left Silver City when he became a teenager, living with one brother or another in Chicago. By age 14 he had reached almost full height. He was strong—and tough. But he was unsupervised and eventually fell into bad company. He began to carry a loaded .22 caliber gun in his pocket. He snatched purses, beat up people, and got into gang fights. It was his revenge for a bitter childhood.

Not everything Spencer did was destructive. He liked most sports, especially basketball. His older brothers were going to college. Spencer's brother Leroy was at Bowling Green. Spencer visited him and spent some time shooting baskets in the college gym. He also got into some games in Detroit. Will Robinson, coach at Pershing High School in Detroit, realized that basketball could be the boy's future. Robinson found a married couple, James and Ida Bell, who agreed to let Spencer live with them while he attended Pershing High.

Spencer blossomed into a basketball and track star at Pershing. College scouts looked him over and were enthusiastic. But his grades were bad and he couldn't qualify for most colleges. Spencer went to junior college, trying to make up for the years of school he had missed. While he was there he became a Junior College All-American. Then came the Olympic tryouts. Spencer showed up and made the team.

So the unheralded American team of "substitutes" went to Mexico City for the Olympics, with only an outside chance of getting to the top. Few people in America realized how hard they had trained, how much faith Hank Iba had in these kids, and how determined they were to show the world what they could do on a basketball court.

The Americans exhibited their brand of play immediately, knocking off Spain,

81–46. Spencer scored 12 points and was the kingpin under the boards.

The Philippines fell to the the U.S. next, 96–75. Then came the tough Yugoslavians. Jo Jo White scored 24 points as the Americans won, 73–58. Now the other countries took notice. The U.S. squad was not going to be a pushover after all.

One after another the competition lost to the rampaging American basketball team. Haywood scored 26 points in their 100–61 victory over Italy. Hard-driving Puerto Rico put up a tussle before bowing, 61–56. Spencer had 21 in that contest. Then Brazil fell, 76–63.

It seemed the final contest would be between America and Russia. But that game was never played. The charged-up Yugoslavs staged one of the greatest upsets in Olympic history, knocking off the Russians by a single point, 63–62.

So it was America against Yugoslavia, again, for the championship. Coach Iba was worried. The Slavs were "up" for the game after their victory over the Russians. And

---

Haywood stuffs the ball decisively in the championship game against Yugoslavia.

U.S. Olympic players and coaches jump off the bench as the final buzzer sounds and the U.S. wins the gold medal.

they had already played the Americans and could take advantage of their weaknesses.

Hank Iba's fears were groundless. The determined band of Americans, realizing that even the superstars could not have done any better, were out to take the gold medal. And they did, 65–50.

The star of that last game was Spencer Haywood. He hustled all over the floor, and his 23 points gave the Americans the margin of victory.

A flock of "second bests" had become the outstanding team in the 1968 Olympics. And a young man named Spencer Haywood put on his own "demonstration" on behalf of black people—by dazzling the world with his skill on a basketball court.

4 · The Small School

In America's Midwest, high-school basketball is more than just a sport—it is almost a religion. This is especially true of the small communities. Teenagers in all parts of the United States love basketball, but when spring comes they usually switch their attention to baseball. Midwestern youngsters like baseball, too, but nothing can induce them to abandon the basketball and hoop completely, regardless of the time of year. A coach in one Minnesota town once remarked, "My boys think of basketball and girls—in that order." And he wasn't kidding!

One of the best examples of a basketball-crazy area is the village of Hebron, Illinois, which is 68 miles northwest of Chicago. In 1952 Hebron had a population of less than 700 people. Hebron High School had an enrollment of 99 students.

Few people would expect such a small school to be a basketball power, but players in *any* Midwestern school can be outstanding. Hebron itself had produced its share of good players and good teams. Back in 1940 little Hebron made it to the state championship tournament, mostly because of Howie Judson. Judson was also a fine pitcher, later playing for the Chicago White Sox.

There were many reasons for the success of Hebron teams over the years. In part it was due to the fans—the parents, teachers, and citizens of the community. When Hebron played a game, the fans were always there to cheer the team on.

Another factor was the coach, Russ Ahearn, who was also the principal. In four years at Hebron (up to 1952) his teams had won 94 games and lost only 15. Ahearn stressed conditioning and strict adherence to the training rules. He insisted that his players eat the right food, date only on Saturday nights, and get to bed early. In the off-season the boys jumped rope, ran four miles a day, and shot baskets for hours in their yards. In practice he stressed the basics: passing, dribbling, shooting, and rebounding. No team in any school, large or small, had better coaching.

Even with sound coaching and the support of their village, the Hebron Green Giants could hardly expect to compete every year. Since one boy of every four in the whole school was needed for the basketball team, it wasn't always easy to pick a solid starting lineup. But the squad for 1951–1952 was remarkable in every way. Hebron High must have had the highest proportion of great basketball players in the country.

Leading the attack were the Judson twins, Paul and Phil. Paul, a 6-foot-3 guard, was the spark plug, while brother Phil, a 6-foot-2 forward, was a fine rebounder and scorer. At center was 6-foot-11 Bill Schulz. Ken Spooner and Don Wilbrandt, two all-round athletes, filled the other two positions.

This Hebron club was a well-coached, high-spirited group. They sailed through the season with only one loss, an upset by Crystal Lake. In the Waukegan regional tournament, Hebron defeated Barrington and DeKalb to qualify for the state championship finals.

On March 20 the Illinois state basketball championship tournament began. Every year the tournament began with the 16 best basketball teams in the state. Many of these teams came from large high schools that had more students than the village of Hebron had people. But the Hebron High team, already considered one of the best in the state, was not intimidated by big-school competition. Hebron took on Champaign in the first round and stunned the afternoon crowd with a great exhibition of fundamental basketball. Only once did Champaign lead—at the very beginning, 4-2. Then Phil and Paul Judson each sank a free throw, and a few moments later Paul tapped in a rebound. The Green Giants were in front to stay. The final score was 55-46.

Hebron and Lawrenceville clashed next, in the semifinals. It was almost no contest. With a great 19-point spurt in the second quarter, Hebron broke the game open and sailed away to a 65-55 win. Now only the powerful Quincy team stood between the Green Giants and the state championship.

In the early part of the game it seemed that Hebron had finally met its match. Quincy poked holes in the Hebron defense, breaking a 6-6 tie and building slowly to a five-point lead. Bruce Brothers, Quincy's 6-foot-5 all-State center, and Dick Thompson, a guard, were doing most of the damage.

A few seconds before the end of the half, Phil and Paul Judson each hit with a basket. But Hebron was still losing, 35–34, when the halftime buzzer sounded.

In the second half, Hebron's Bill Schulz was a tower of strength under the boards, pulling down one rebound after another. He was scoring too. Yet the Quincy Blue Devils refused to quit. At the end of three periods the game was tied, 48–all.

Then in the fourth quarter Hebron edged slowly out in front by six points. Again Quincy stormed back. Dick Thompson hit with a pair of clutch free throws, Chuck Fast got another, and Tom Paynes scored with a jump shot to cut Hebron's margin to one point. Then Bill Schulz gave his team some breathing room with a layup, and Hebron clung grimly to its lead until there was just over a minute to play. At that point Quincy's Jack Gower broke through with a basket. Ten seconds later the score was tied when Quincy's Gower flipped in a foul shot.

In the final seconds Quincy might have pulled the game out, as they had done frequently in the past, but the determined Hebron defense blocked Quincy's shots. The buzzer sounded with the score tied, 58–all. It was the first overtime championship game in the history of the tournament.

Twenty seconds into the extra session it was virtually all over. Bill Schulz drove in for a layup, and a minute later Phil Judson did the same thing. Wilbrandt scored with a free throw and so did Phil Judson. Quincy could only manage a single point, and Hebron won, 64–59.

There was no individual hero on the Hebron team. Bill Schulz was high scorer with 24 points, but the five Hebron starters had won the entire game together. Quincy had been durable, too, using just one sub, and then only because Bruce Brothers had fouled out.

The Chicago *Tribune* called the contest "one of the greatest final games in history." The paper also ran a column on its editorial page praising the boys and the tiny town of Hebron. State police escorted the victory caravan back to Hebron. There were 40 cars when the procession began and 600 cars at the finish. Thousands of fans from Hebron and the surrounding towns swarmed around outside while the players were being interviewed by a local radio station inside Joe's Barber Shop. It was a heartwarming scene for the smallest school ever to win the championship.

5·Buddies

It was the final game of the 1958 season for the Minneapolis Lakers and the Cincinnati Royals. The game meant little to the Lakers, for they had been eliminated from the play-offs. But the Royals had won a spot in the post-season series, and they were playing hard, preparing for the tough games ahead.

Most of the fans were watching Maurice "Big Mo" Stokes, Cincinnati's great sharp-shooter. Two years before he had been Rookie of the Year, and during the 1958 season he had already scored more than 1,000 points. Stokes was having his usual hot game when suddenly he tripped and fell, hitting his head on the hardwood floor. He was knocked unconscious and didn't come to for several minutes.

"How are you feeling, Mo?" asked team-mate Jack Twyman.

"I've felt better," muttered Stokes. He then grinned sheepishly and said, "I just needed a little sleep, that's all."

Three days later, in Detroit, the Royals played and lost to the Pistons in a semifinal playoff game. Stokes played hard, but he did not shoot well, scoring only a dozen points. He also complained of headaches.

On the plane back to Cincinnati, Big Mo suddenly lapsed into a coma. When the plane landed, he was rushed to the hospital. Doctors were puzzled at first. They didn't know of the tumble he took in the Minneapolis game, for that had happened three days before and Stokes seemed to have recovered. When the doctors were told of Mo's fall, they took X rays of his head. They soon discovered that the motor-control center of his brain was badly damaged.

Maurice Stokes was paralyzed. The doctors said he would be unable to move or talk for the rest of his life.

Jack Twyman and Maurice Stokes had never been the best of friends. They had been teammates and had enjoyed joking with each other, but that was about all. However, when he learned how badly Stokes had been injured, Twyman went into action.

Stokes would have to remain in the hospital for many years—perhaps for the rest of his life. Twyman knew that Mo didn't have

Playing in his last game, on March 16, 1958, Maurice Stokes guards Detroit's George Yardley.

the money to pay for the doctors, nurses, medicine, and hospital room. So Twyman persuaded the NBA to stage a benefit game to raise money for his former teammate.

On October 21, 1958, the first Maurice

Stokes benefit game was played, and some of basketball's greatest stars participated. The game raised $10,000, and even the players had to pay to get into the arena.

Twyman realized, however, that Stokes needed more than money. He needed the will to continue living. Twyman visited his former teammate often. At first Twyman did all the talking, but after a while they worked out a system so that Mo could respond. Twyman would recite the alphabet, and when he came to the letter Stokes wanted to use, Mo would blink his eyes. They repeated this routine over and over, spelling out what Mo wanted to say. It was a long process, slow and painful, but at least Big Mo was communicating with his friend.

Then Maurice began to learn how to talk again. He had to start with the basics, first sounding the vowels and then simple words like "cat" and "dog" and "yes." This, too, was a slow, slow process, but he refused to quit. Eventually he began to say words with more than one syllable.

Sometimes his eyes would bulge as he strained to get the words out of his mouth. Jack Twyman stayed by his side, encouraging and goading him to greater efforts. Once

Stokes actually spit as he tried to say a tough word. Twyman wiped his face and asked, "Hey, Mo, do you supply towels with your showers?"

Finally he began to say whole sentences. He said them slowly and with long pauses, but he said them. And Twyman was there to joke with him, to tease him, and to keep Mo's spirits up.

"Hey, Mo, I was a better college player than you," needled Twyman. "Remember when we played against each other? I scored one point more in that game than you did."

"Jack . . ." gasped Stokes, "you're . . . always . . . bragging . . . about . . . that. . . . I . . . wasn't . . . feeling . . . well . . . that . . . day."

Now that Stokes could speak, he began physical therapy to gain some small amount of movement. He learned to make ceramic objects, and they were good too! After one Maurice Stokes benefit game, Big Mo gave each player an ashtray or a vase as a token of his appreciation.

But most of the ceramics went to Jack Twyman, who could not resist joking with Stokes about them.

"You sign those things with your initials,

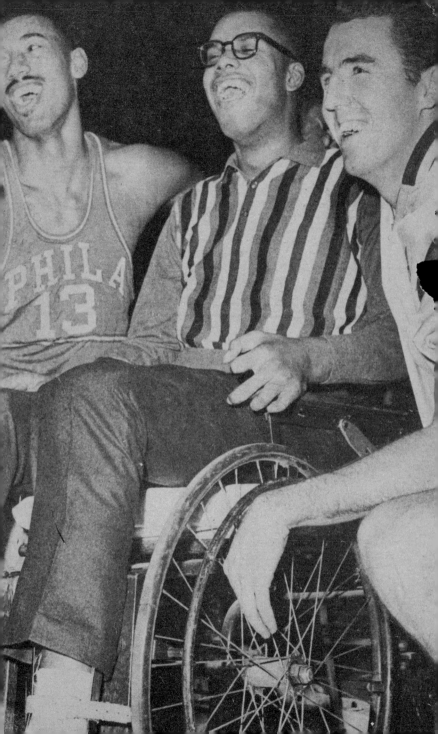

'M.S.' Who do you think you are, Picasso?"

Stokes grinned and replied, "Picasso . . . never . . . played . . . forward."

In 1967 Maurice Stokes attended his benefit game. A plane was hired to take him from Cincinnati to the resort in New York State where the game was played. As he was wheeled out onto the court in a wheelchair, the sellout crowd and the players stood and cheered. His courage and fighting spirit had touched the hearts of thousands.

Maurice Stokes died in 1970. The Maurice Stokes benefit game is still held every year, but the proceeds now go to another charity.

Jack Twyman had helped Stokes in his need, but Big Mo was not the only one to benefit. Twyman himself had gained quite a bit.

"You know," he said, "whenever I felt down in the dumps about something, I'd visit Mo. He always cheered me up. I've become a better person because of that man."

Wilt Chamberlain, Stokes, and Twyman pose for photographers at a Cincinnati Royals game in January 1960. Stokes is out of the hospital here for the first time in nearly two years.

6·Basketball's Highest Scorer

Rio Grande College, a tiny school in Ohio, had an enrollment of 94 full-time students in 1952. One of these students was named Bevo, a 6-foot-9 freshman whose real name was Clarence Francis. Before Bevo came to Rio Grande, very few people had heard of either one. But by the time he left, both Rio Grande College and Bevo were practically household words—at least for basketball fans.

Bevo had learned how to shoot a basketball in a barn, where he had nailed a hoop to a wall. By the time he decided to get a college education, he had a deadly accurate shot. But he also had a wife and son and no high-school diploma. Nevertheless, he tried to get into Rio Grande College. It seemed doubtful that he would make it, but once coach Newt Oliver saw Bevo's towering figure and accurate shooting, he was accepted.

It was not long before Bevo and Rio Grande College began to be noticed. In a game against Ashland Junior College of Kentucky, Bevo scored an incredible 116 points. Of course, Rio Grande won, 150–85.

With Bevo Francis in the lineup, Rio Grande College took off on a fantastic winning streak, ringing up astronomical scores. By the end of the season Rio Grande had won 39 in a row. Even more startling were the figures compiled by Bevo.

During the 1952–1953 season Rio Grande had scored the staggering total of 3,964 points. Bevo had accounted for 1,954 of those points! His average was an unbelieveable 50.1 points per game!

Bevo's record was easily the best in college basketball. But the National Collegiate Athletic Association decided that even though Bevo was a high scorer, his records were not official because Rio Grande's opponents were too weak. Most of them were junior college, seminary, or military post teams.

Although Rio Grande was upset over the NCAA ruling, the team started the next season just as it had ended the previous one.

Again Bevo was outstanding. In a game against Alliance College he scored 84 points. Then he went "over the top" a second time, scoring 113 points against Hillsdale. By then everyone wanted to see this hot-shot in action against good competition. So tiny Rio Grande was booked into Madison Square Garden in New York City, the home of big-college basketball.

Rio Grande played Adelphi and lost, 83–76. Bevo didn't do too badly. He scored 32 points, but they were all scored in the first half. In the second half he was covered by four players. Time and again his teammates were open but they couldn't sink a shot. Perhaps they became flustered because Bevo usually took all the shots. Then Rio Grande lost to Villanova. But Bevo scored 39 points and it was a close game all the way.

Sportswriters, seeing the famous Bevo for the first time, realized that he was still untrained. He didn't move around much but stayed instead in the pivot post and did a lot of shooting. Yet he had a marvelous touch. He flicked the ball effortlessly toward the basket, and usually the ball went in.

Finally the boys from Ohio won against

a big-time opponent, Providence College. Bevo scored 41 points.

In 1953–1954 Bevo scored 1,254 points in 27 games for a 46.5 average. Both the United Press and the Associated Press named him to their second team for All-American honors. It was only his second year, and he seemed to be on his way to bigger and better things. He might even have gone to a bigger school, where he would get more recognition.

Then, suddenly, Bevo Francis was no longer in any college. He was expelled from school because he had missed too many classes and failed to make up midterm exams that he had missed. Bevo said that he would have had to quit school anyway because he was almost out of money and the bills were piling up.

Coach Newt Oliver was enraged and declared that if Bevo quit he would leave Rio Grande too. That was exactly what happened.

Abe Saperstein, owner of the Harlem Globetrotters, signed both Bevo and Oliver to a joint contract with the Boston Whirlwinds, which Saperstein also owned. Bevo played pro basketball for a while but he

Bevo Francis (right) and his coach, Newt Oliver (center), count the money they received from Abe Saperstein (left) for signing a contract with Saperstein's Boston Whirlwinds.

never got very far. Soon he dropped out of sight.

Rio Grande College has also dropped out

of sight. Its basketball team has gone back to playing unknown opponents. And without the heroics of Bevo Francis the team is no longer mentioned in the circles of big-time basketball.

7·Bob Pettit
Comes Through

The seventh game of the 1956–1957 play-offs between the Boston Celtics and the St. Louis Hawks was one of the most exciting basketball games ever played. They battled point for point the entire game. Then, with just three seconds left, the Hawks were losing by two points and their star, Bob Pettit, was fouled. The pressure was enormous, but the sharpshooting forward stepped to the free-throw line and sank two foul shots to tie the game.

The first overtime period produced more great action. With only four seconds to go, the Hawks' Jack Coleman sank a long one to knot the score again.

The bone-tired players kept firing away through the second overtime, and the lead changed hands a couple of times. Boston's Frank Ramsey put his team three points ahead near the end of the period, but little

Slater Martin, St. Louis' 5-foot-10 guard, made a free throw to cut the margin to two points.

One by one players on both sides had fouled out. The Hawks had lost four men, and player-coach Alex Hannum was forced to put himself in the game.

With only three seconds left to go, the Hawks, losing by two points, had the ball out of bounds. Hannum and Bob Pettit set up one last play, hoping to tie the score once again.

The ball was passed in to Hannum. He let fly with a desperation heave at the basket. Meanwhile, Pettit was streaking downcourt. As Hannum's throw reached the backboard Pettit hurled himself up into the air. His fingertips brushed against the ball, knocking it toward the basket. As the buzzer sounded the ball hung on the rim for a heart-stopping split-second—then dropped out. After several valiant comebacks the Hawks had fallen short, losing the game and the NBA championship.

Bob Pettit blamed himself for the loss. "I should have tapped it in," he said sadly. "Nobody was near me. I should have made the shot."

"No way!" Hannum disagreed loudly. "I'll never understand how you got so far downcourt in the first place. Nobody else could have gotten close. Don't blame yourself, because it *wasn't* your fault."

But Pettit refused to be comforted. In his mind he was responsible, even though all his teammates thought otherwise. "We'll get 'em next year," Pettit muttered.

Next year came. The Hawks and the Celtics made it to the finals again in 1958, and they tore into each other just as they had done the season before. Bob Pettit played as if the entire series were his responsibility.

In the first game Pettit's final basket gave the Hawks a 104–102 victory. He had scored 30 points. In the second game he was held to 18 points as the Celtics came roaring back to win, 136–112.

In the third game Pettit broke through again. Time and again the Celtics fell behind, and every time they narrowed the margin, Pettit sank another bucket. In the third period alone he scored 18 points, and the Hawks won, 111–108.

Pettit defends against Cincinnati's Jack Twyman in November 1959.

The champion Celtics were riddled with injuries, but they knew that they had to stop Bob Pettit—and his sidekick, Cliff Hagan—if they were to stay in the series. Pettit was double-teamed throughout game four and could manage only 12 points. The Hawks lost, 109–98.

Nobody could hold Bob Pettit in the fifth game, however. Although he didn't shoot the winning basket in the Hawks' 102–100 victory, he was high-point man with 33.

The Hawks knew that even with injuries the Celtics were dangerous. They had to win the sixth game, for if the Celtics won they might have enough momentum and fighting spirit to win it all in the seventh. Bob Pettit especially wanted to win. He could not forget the bitter defeat of the previous year.

There was something unreal about the Hawks and the Celtics' next encounter. Both teams played as if it were the last game they would ever play. Pettit scored the first basket on a 20-foot jump shot and then kept dropping them in until he had 12 points in the first period. But the Celts had stayed close, and the Hawks only led by four at the break.

In the second period Pettit kept up the pressure, scoring nine more points. But the fighting Celtics refused to quit, and at the half they trailed by only five points, 57–52.

The third period was more of the same. Pettit was hitting from fantastic angles, dropping in six baskets in as many tries. But the Celtics hung on in spite of Pettit. Although the Hawks were ahead by seven when the last period started, the ballgame was far from finished.

Boston put out a do-or-die effort, storming back to tie it up. Then the Celtics' Lou Tsioropolous hit with the basket that sent Boston out in front.

Bob Pettit responded to this threat magnificently. He was a one-man gang, covering the whole court as if it were his private property. With six minutes to go, his basket put the Hawks ahead. And when the Celts streaked back, Pettit was there with another clutch shot. It seemed he couldn't miss.

With 16 seconds to go, the Hawks led by only a single point. They got the ball, and backcourt man Slater Martin shot for what he hoped would be insurance points—but he missed.

Even as the ball was bouncing off the rim, the memory of Alex Hannum's missed shot the previous year burned in Bob Pettit's brain. With a tremendous effort he out-jumped the Celtics' 6-foot-10 Arnie Risen, tipping the ball up—and in.

Then St. Louis permitted Bill Sharman of Boston to drive in for an easy layup. The Hawks were not about to foul Sharman and give him the chance to tie the score.

Only seconds were left as Slater Martin dribbled out the clock. Boston tried frantically to get their hands on the ball, but it was too late. St. Louis won, 110–109, and became the NBA champions!

So Bob Pettit atoned for an error he never committed. He made a last-second tip-in shot—the same shot he had missed the previous year—to beat the Boston Celtics and gain his revenge.

8 · The High and Low of Pro Basketball

Modern pro basketball is a fast, high-scoring game. It is not unusual for each team in a game to roll up more than 100 points. The players shoot often and with great accuracy. And the rules of modern basketball promote large scores—a pro team may only hold the ball 24 seconds before taking a shot. But in its earlier days basketball was much different.

In 1916 a community house formed an amateur basketball team called the Original Celtics. Two years later the team turned professional and beat just about every team it faced. At about that same time a New York promoter named Tex Rickard formed a club, the Whirlwinds, and it too was outstanding. The two teams met in a two-game series to determine which was the best team in basketball, but the meeting ended in a draw. The Whirlwinds won the first encounter, 40–27, while the Celtics took the second game, 26–24.

These were basketball's best shooters, and yet the scores were relatively low by modern standards. One reason for that was that there was a center jump after every basket and foul shot. So much time was wasted controlling the tap and forming the attack.

In the 1930s the center jump after a score was eliminated and the present rule was enacted. After one team scored, the other team put the ball in play from out of bounds. In that way the game was speeded up and scores rose dramatically. Soon even college teams could score 60 or more points per game, and by 1950 pro teams were hitting the 100-point mark frequently.

In 1950 the outstanding professional basketball team was the Minneapolis Lakers. One player dominated the scene—the Lakers' George Mikan, a 6-foot-10 sharpshooter who played a great defensive game too. His teammates Jim Pollard, Vern Mikkelsen, and Slater Martin were also outstanding. The Lakers scored with such ease that opposing teams decided that the only way to beat Minneapolis was to stall—they would keep the ball out of the Lakers' hands and shoot only when they were sure of hitting.

Several teams tried that strategy, but with little success. Somehow the Lakers always edged into the lead, forcing the other team to take more shots. Mikan then gobbled up the rebounds, and the Lakers simply increased their lead and steadily pulled away.

Still, a few teams continued to use the stall despite its consistent failure. On November 22, 1950, the Lakers played the Fort Wayne (now Detroit) Pistons. Right from the start the Pistons put on the stall. Undoubtedly Minneapolis was by then familiar with that tactic. But somehow Fort Wayne's slow play upset them, and they missed a number of golden scoring opportunities. The home-town Laker fans began to hoot, jeer, whistle, and stomp, but the Pistons stuck doggedly to their game plan.

At the end of the first period Fort Wayne led, 8–7. They clung to their slight edge for most of the second period, until Mikan put his club ahead, 11–10, with less than two minutes to go in the half. At halftime Minneapolis led, 13–11.

The third period was equally incredible. Fort Wayne scored five points, but the

Lakers scored four and held on to the lead, 17–16. By then the fans were loudly complaining that they weren't getting their money's worth. But there was nothing the referee could do—everything the Pistons were doing was absolutely legal.

The fourth quarter was the strangest of them all. Only four points were scored the entire period. And although most of the game was dull, the last few seconds were wildly exciting. With only nine seconds left, the Lakers were ahead, 18–17. Fort Wayne's Larry Foust drove in and shot over the outstretched arms of George Mikan. It was only Foust's second shot of the game—and it was good!

With about five seconds left, Slater Martin got the ball, drove downcourt, and threw a desperation shot at the basket. But the ball hit the rim and bounced away just as the final horn sounded. The Lakers had scored only one point that period, while the Pistons scored three to win the game, 19–18.

A number of records were set that day, including fewest shots and fewest points in a quarter, a half, and a game. The only Laker to score a field goal was George Mikan, who had only four baskets in the game. Mikan also made seven free throws and was high scorer in the game, with 15 of his team's 18 points. The number of personal fouls in the game was also low—the Lakers had a team total of 11 and the Pistons had 14.

Pro basketball fans and NBA officials were enraged about the game, and sportswriters complained about the lack of action. Maurice Podoloff, president of the NBA, said grimly, "It'll never happen again!"

And it didn't. The pros soon adopted the 24-second rule, providing that the team with the ball must shoot within 24 seconds or give up the ball to the other team.

After that the high scorers took command of basketball. And although there were plenty of good defensive players, they couldn't contain marksmen like Paul Arizin, Jerry West, Elgin Baylor, and Wilt Chamberlain. All were capable of scoring better than 40 points per game, and frequently they did just that.

One night, against the New York Knicks, Elgin Baylor scored 71 points. After the game he was asked how long he thought his record would last. "Just a short time," Baylor replied. "Almost anytime now Wilt Chamberlain will hit 100 points."

Nobody laughed at Baylor's remark. The 100-point mark had been hit before, but only in a college game. Everyone knew that if that feat was ever to be duplicated, Chamberlain was the one to do it.

On March 2, 1962, the Philadelphia 76ers, with Wilt Chamberlain, took the floor against the New York Knicks at Hershey, Pennsylvania. A crowd of 4,124 small-town basketball fans jammed the arena.

Only a month before, Chamberlain had scored 78 points in a game, surpassing Baylor's mark of 71. Chamberlain was hot this night, too, and the fans sensed it immediately. Every one-hander, every fall-away shot, went through the net as though the ball had eyes. He was even hitting on his free throws, which he usually made less than 50 percent of the time.

As the game went into the fourth quarter the fans were standing up, screaming "Give it to Wilt!" every time a Philadelphia player got the ball. Chamberlain had already surpassed his record of 78 points, but the fans wanted to see him score as many as he could.

Chamberlain sinks another two-pointer to set a scoring record in a game against the New York Knicks in 1962.

The Knicks tried desperately to stop Wilt. Darrall Imhoff, who had tried to defend against him, fouled out in the final period. The Knicks then tried to gang up on Wilt, but it was no use.

Seconds before the game ended, Wilt Chamberlain hit his one-hundredth point! Of course, Philadelphia won—169–147!

Wilt's 100 points were, of course, a new mark. He also set records for most points scored by one man in a quarter and in a half. The total score by both teams—316 points—eclipsed the old mark of 312 points.

Basketball had come a long way. In the game between the Lakers and the Pistons in 1950, the total points scored was only 37. In this Philadelphia-New York game Wilt Chamberlain himself scored 39 points—in the first quarter alone.

9·Stallworth Returns

Basketball is running, jumping, shooting, twisting, turning, bending, shoving, falling, tripping, elbowing—and more running. In short, basketball is not the ideal game for someone with a heart condition.

On March 7, 1967, Dave Stallworth, a promising young player on the New York Knicks, suddenly felt pains in his chest. He had not been ill before, so there was really no warning. He was practicing a few easy hook shots before an away game when suddenly he felt as if someone were sitting on his chest.

The thought of a heart attack never entered his mind. He thought instead that the pains were caused by indigestion. Just to be on the safe side Stallworth was examined by a doctor, who found nothing wrong with him. He was told it was all right to play that night, but that when he returned to New York his physician should give him a thorough examination.

Nevertheless, Stallworth didn't play much

that night. Although the chest pains had disappeared, he stayed out because of a minor leg injury. It turned out to be the luckiest bruise he had ever received, for the extra exertion might have killed him! Two days later, back in New York, a specialist checked him thoroughly. When the tests were examined, Stallworth wasn't even permitted to return home. He went directly from the doctor's office to the hospital.

At the age of 25 and seemingly in top condition, Dave Stallworth had suffered a heart attack. It had been a narrow escape. Doctors were amazed that he had gone through part of a rough basketball game and survived two days more.

Stallworth was in the hospital for 27 days, most of the time flat on his back. Even before the doctors talked to him, he could read the handwriting on the wall—his basketball days were over. He knew that the game was much too strenuous for a heart patient.

After his release from the hospital, Stallworth returned home to recuperate. He enrolled in a few courses at Wichita State University. The doctors had prescribed mild exercise, so he played golf and took long walks. He did some scouting for the Knicks, had regular checkups, and resigned himself to a new way of life.

But the call of the basketball court was too strong to resist forever. As his health improved he began to fool around with the ball in schoolyards. At first he would shoot a few baskets from the foul line. Then gradually he worked his way back to shooting the ball from 25 feet out. He tried to talk some kids into feeding him the ball for some easy layups, but the youngsters were afraid that would cause another heart attack.

Stallworth was not telling his doctors what he was doing. He fooled them—which might not have been very smart—by resting before checkups so that the doctors detected no strain when they listened to his heart with a stethoscope.

When he finally did admit his activity, the medics were astonished. Dave Stallworth had recovered completely! He had taken it easy at first, improving his health slowly. The amazed doctors told him he could resume his basketball career.

The Knicks welcomed Dave Stallworth back with open arms. He began to work out with the team, fitting himself into the plays again. He substituted in exhibition games, averaging about 10 points per game. After a while his timing was sharper, his rebounding was more forceful, and his passes were right on the mark.

On opening day 1969, thirty-one months after his heart attack, Stallworth was back in Madison Square Garden. The players lined up at the entrance to the court, ready to race out to the floor as their names were announced. The first name called was Dave Stallworth.

As the reserve forward trotted out into the glare of the lights, thousands of fans rose to their feet and applauded. Stallworth stood quietly, hands behind his back, as his teammates came out onto the court one by one to take their places beside him.

The first Knick sub to get into the game was Stallworth. He didn't do much in the first half, but soon the nervousness and stiffness wore off. In the second half he hit three jump shots, grabbed half a dozen rebounds, and stole the ball three times. It was the Dave Stallworth of old, playing up to his full potential.

Stallworth soars high above his defenders to score an important two points in a 1970 playoff game.

The Knicks won the championship that year, and Stallworth played an important role, coming off the bench to score key baskets. In the playoff finals, when Knick center Willis Reed was injured, Stallworth and Dave DeBusschere filled in at center, guarding big Wilt Chamberlain. The championship was a team victory, and Dave Stallworth contributed as much as any Knick.

Athletes have come back from many illnesses and injuries. But there was something special about a man who could play professional basketball after recovering from a heart attack!

10 · The Wrong Sub

Basketball officials have numerous rules to enforce, many of them requiring split-second decisions. A good example is the three-second rule. When a team is in possession of the ball, none of its players can remain inside the opposing team's foul lane more than three seconds. An official must have a "stopwatch brain" to keep track of the players as they weave in and out of the foul lane.

Officials also find it difficult to keep track of substitutions. Sometimes they make mistakes. One glaring error took place during a 1952 semifinal playoff game between the New York Knicks and the Boston Celtics.

The Knicks were leading, 79–76, in a hard-fought contest. With two minutes left, Knick coach Joe Lapchick sent backcourt man Dick McGuire to the scorer's bench to report that he was going in for Ray Lumpp.

McGuire didn't report in right away, waiting for the action on the court to stop. In the meantime his teammate Max Zaslofsky fouled Bob Cousy. It was Zaslofsky's sixth personal foul, and he was out of the game. Coach Lapchick told Nat "Sweetwater" Clifton to replace Zaslofsky.

In those days, after a player sank a foul shot with two minutes or less to play, a jump ball was held between the shooter and the man who fouled him (or his substitute). The Knicks wanted desperately to gain contol of the ball, and they figured Sweetwater Clifton, who was almost half a foot taller than Cousy, would win the tap.

But the officials got things mixed up. Instead of McGuire for Lumpp and Clifton for Zaslofsky, the officials had it McGuire for Zaslofsky and Clifton for Lumpp.

In most situations this wouldn't have mattered. The two subs could guard anybody they pleased, and the officials would not care. But this was not an ordinary situation. The jump ball was coming up, matching Dick McGuire, Zaslofsky's official substitute, against Bob Cousy. Both were about the same height, and either one might control the tap.

Lapchick was off the Knick bench in an instant, screaming at the officials. "No! No! McGuire is replacing *Lumpp,* not Zaslofsky.

Didn't you see him at the scorer's bench a couple of seconds ago?"

The officials considered Lapchick's objection and then reversed their decision. But Red Auerbach was no fool. He knew the Knicks would have the advantage if Clifton jumped against Cousy, so he bounced up and shouted that the original decision must stand. Confused, the officials reversed themselves again.

Lapchick grew more angry and protested. The officials reversed themselves a third time. Auerbach was furious, and for the fourth time, the officials reversed their decision.

The argument raged back and forth until finally the officials had had enough. Auerbach won the dispute, and Lapchick lost.

Bob Cousy outjumped Dick McGuire, and the Celtics gained possession and tied the score with a last-second shot.

The game went into overtime, and it seemed that the Celtics had won the game when Cousy scored on a 40-foot heave. But the officials ruled that the basket was made after the buzzer and therefore didn't count. It was then Auerbach's turn to rant and rave at the "dunderheaded" officials, but this time they stood firm.

The game went into a second overtime period, and the Knicks pulled it out with two seconds left on Ernie Vandeweghe's bucket. New York had won after all.

Still, that game proved that an official's job is thankless—some days he can't please anybody!

11·Basketball's Longest Games

There is an old cliché in sports: "Somebody has to win and somebody has to lose." Except for regular-season hockey and football games, which can end in ties, this is true. But there have been some games, in all sports, that went hours into overtime before winners were decided.

Many basketball games have gone into one overtime period, and even two extra periods is not too unusual. But for a game to go into a third extra period is pretty rare. Still, there have been games that have gone into a fourth and fifth overtime. Only four games, however, have ever extended into a sixth overtime period.

All four of these games were college matches. On February 21, 1953, Niagara University played Siena College at Albany, New York. It was a tight game right down to the wire. The score was tied, 54–all, and

The starting five of Niagara University's 1953 team. Eddie Fleming, who played the entire extra-overtime game, is number 70.

there were only a few seconds left when Gerry Kennedy of Niagara took the ball down the sideline and let go with a one-hander on the run. It swished in. But even before Kennedy shot, there was a commotion in the stands and on the sidelines. The Siena timer was saying that the clock had run out before Kennedy shot. The Niagara timer disagreed, saying that the ball was in the air when the game ended. The referee said that he didn't hear the buzzer.

The two sides argued for ten minutes, and finally the referee declared that the basket didn't count.

In the first overtime each team scored 7 points. After a rest they played the second overtime, each team ringing up only two points. The game went into a third, fourth, fifth, and sixth extra period before Niagara finally pulled it out, 88–81. The game had consumed three hours and two minutes.

A six-overtime game is strange enough, but there was an additional oddity about this one. Niagara's Eddie Fleming played the *entire 70 minutes* of basketball! Afterward, his jersey number was changed to 70 in honor of his feat. The period line-score read like this:

Niagara: 25 29 7 2 7 2 4 12 = 88
Siena: 24 30 7 2 7 2 4 5 = 81

On December 13, 1954, Western Illinois

University and St. Ambrose College went at it in Macomb, Illinois. St. Ambrose led by two with just four seconds left to play. Then Western Illinois called a time-out to set up a desperation play. When play resumed, the ball was passed in to Lupe Rios, who tossed it on the run to Charles Schramm. Schramm let fly with a 45-footer, and it went in! The buzzer sounded and the game was tied, 51–51.

The play that followed was one of the most unbelievable series of overtimes in basketball history. Both teams tried to freeze the ball, so that they could score in the final seconds of the period. But both teams missed their last-minute shots. In six overtimes Western Illinois scored only seven points and St. Ambrose only six! In three of the overtimes neither team scored at all! Western Illinois won, 58–57:

Western Illinois: 22 29 2 3 0 0 0 2 = 58
St. Ambrose: 31 20 2 3 0 0 0 1 = 57

On January 29, 1955, Purdue University and the University of Minnesota played to a 57–57 tie at the end of regulation time. Then followed some of the most frustrating minutes in the history of basketball. The defense

74

on both sides was superb, and both teams played so carefully that spectators blinked their eyes in disbelief.

For four consecutive overtime periods neither team scored!

In the fifth extra period each team scored only two points. But it was becoming obvious that someone was going to break the game open.

Finally, in the sixth period, Purdue grabbed a three-point lead. From the way the teams had scored before, those three points seemed to be more than enough. But then Purdue got careless. A bad out-of-bounds pass gave the ball to Minnesota, and the Gophers scored a basket. Purdue turned the ball over to Minnesota again when one of its players double-dribbled. The Gophers scored again, taking the lead. Purdue was completely demoralized, and Minnesota scored four more points. When it was just about over, Purdue scored once more. But by then it made no difference. Minnesota won, 59–56.

This was undoubtedly the most carefully played game in college history, especially considering its length. Each team used only six players. Only one player, Ted Dunn of

Purdue, fouled out. Minnesota players committed 15 fouls, and Purdue had only 11. The period score:

Minnesota: 23 24 0 0 0 0 2 10 = 59
Purdue: 27 20 0 0 0 0 2 7 = 56

On January 5, 1957, Coe College and Monmouth College played an extra-long basketball game at Cedar Rapids, Iowa. Monmouth appeared to have won the game, but in the closing seconds Al Pursell of Coe stole the ball and scored on a driving layup to knot the score at 52–52.

After that it was the same old cautious, low-scoring defensive game. In five consecutive periods each team scored only two points.

For a while it looked like the record for the longest game would be broken—the sixth overtime period was almost over and neither team had scored. In the last minute of the extra session Don Huff of Coe broke through the Monmouth defense to score on a layup. And he was fouled in the act of shooting. Huff went to the free-throw line and scored the one-pointer. That ended the scoring. Coe foiled a desperate Monmouth scoring attempt, then gained possession of the ball and ran the time out. The final score was 65–62. The period score:

Coe: 24 28 2 2 2 2 2 3 = 65
Monmouth: 28 24 2 2 2 2 2 0 = 62

12 · The Champions

Every year after the regular college basketball season there are two big tournaments for top college teams. The NCAA tournament is sponsored by the National Collegiate Athletic Association, and the teams in the championship series are chosen in regional playoffs. The other tournament, the National Invitational Tournament (NIT), is held every year in New York's Madison Square Garden, and some of the best teams in the country are invited. The problem is that the two tournaments are played at the same time, so no team can compete in both. Basketball fans have often argued about which team in a given year was better—the NCAA winner or the NIT winner. The issue could not be settled because after the tournaments the teams went home and the college basketball season was officially over.

It wasn't always that way. Years ago the NIT was held earlier, and a team that made the NIT finals was often invited to the

NCAA championships. In that way it was possible for a team to win both and become undisputed national champion—but until 1950 this never happened.

In 1950 the teams in the NIT were the finest in the nation. For instance, the Kentucky Wildcats, coached by the great Adolph Rupp, had racked up a 14-game winning streak, sparked by their seven-foot center, Bill Spivey. Bradley University boasted a pair of standout players in Paul Unruh and Gene Melchiorre and won the championship in the Missouri Valley Conference. Another team that was invited was City College of New York. Although CCNY seemed to be a good, sound team, no one thought it would get very far.

As a rule City College teams were better than average. And the coach, Nat Holman, was one of the best in the history of basketball. But the players, though good enough to make any team in the country, were interested in more than basketball. They attended CCNY mainly to get an education. In fact, the City College team had the best scholars of any squad in the country.

CCNY was a free school, but to get in, a student had to hold at least a B-minus average through high school and pass a stiff entrance examination. In addition, a student had to maintain a C average at CCNY or be dropped from school.

Even though studying demanded a great deal of the players' time, CCNY had had some truly remarkable basketball teams. From 1922 through 1925 CCNY won 36 games and lost only 4! And during another three-year stretch, from 1931 through 1934, CCNY won 43 and lost only 3!

By the 1949–1950 season Nat Holman had been coaching at CCNY for 30 years. His team that year was composed mostly of sophomores, including Ed Roman at center, Ed Warner and Arnold Smith at forward, and Herb Cohen, Floyd Layne, and Alvin Roth at guard. Roman, Warner, and Roth were starters, and the rest were subs.

The City College Beavers started the season well, reeling off five straight victories. But only one of those wins was against tough opposition. City beat Southern Methodist University, 67–53.

Then the inexperienced Beavers began to flounder a bit. They lost to Oklahoma by four points but recovered in the next game to trounce California. Then they lost to UCLA,

Coach Nat Holman (front, center) and the 1949–1950 City College of New York basketball team.

60–53, after leading through the first half of the game.

This was only a temporary setback, however. City took on a strong St. John's team, which had won twelve in a row, and beat them, 54–52. They followed that win with six victories in a row.

Once again CCNY turned sour, losing two in a row, to Canisius and Niagara. Then the Beavers won two, against St. Joseph's and Fordham, before losing to a hot Syracuse team, 83–74. The team was inexperienced, and it showed in the games against top competition.

City ended the year with triumphs over its traditional rivals, Manhattan and New York University, to post a season record of 17 wins and 5 losses. Since it had gone undefeated in local competition and had become New York's "Subway Conference" champion—beating its local New York City rivals—City College received an invitation to the NIT.

Although CCNY had beaten Princeton, the Ivy League champs, and routed a good Muhlenberg squad by 29 points in the regular season, the Beavers were not expected to get past their first NIT game. Their first opponent was to be the defending NIT champion, San Francisco University.

The City College boys surprised everyone in that first game, knocking off San Francisco, 65–46. But their next opponent, Kentucky, was the previous season's NCAA champion and was riding a 14-game winning streak. Kentucky's coach, Adolph Rupp, called this team his finest ever, better even than his former championship teams.

It was a slaughter! After four and a half minutes City led, 13–1. At the 11:25 mark the score was 28–9. By halftime the stunned Kentucky Wildcats were on the short end of a 45–20 score. Throughout the first half Ed Roman had limited Kentucky's big Bill Spivey, the seven-foot center, to exactly three shots at the basket!

The second half was much like the first, and the final score was 89–50. Never before had a Rupp-coached team received such a drubbing.

Two nights later the kids from CCNY toppled a tough Duquesne team, 62–52. Only then did they receive an invitation to the NCAA tournament to be held after the NIT was over.

But the NIT wasn't over yet. The Braves from Bradley University were City's opponents in the finals, and there the streak seemed about to end.

The first half was a nightmare for Nat Holman's boys. They missed easy layups and seven out of eight free throws. Still, Bradley led by only three points at the half.

Somehow City had stayed close, fighting back in short rallies.

It was different in the second half. CCNY came storming back, and they didn't miss their shots. They took the lead and staved off repeated attempts by the Braves to catch up. City pulled away to win, 69–61. They were NIT champs!

New York City went wild over its underdog heroes. There were celebrations at the college and in Times Square. A resolution of congratulations was passed by the City Council, and the team was greeted personally by Mayor William O'Dwyer. Then it went on to the NCAA tournament.

Ohio State, champion of the powerful Big Ten, was City's first opponent. It was a rough, bruising game. The Buckeyes, led by All-American Dick Schnitker, battled the Beavers point for point. Ohio's zone defense was keeping City stars Warner and Roman bottled up. At the half the score was tied, 40–all.

City found the right combination in the low-scoring second half. Floyd Layne and

Ed Warner of CCNY scores a layup against Bradley University in the NIT finals.

85

Norm Mager shot from the outside, popping the ball in over the Buckeyes' zone defense. In a hard-driving finish City squeaked through by a single point, 56–55.

North Carolina State, another excellent team, was next. The squad was led by two of the best players in the nation, Dick Dickey and Sam Ranzino. The game was close, but again the Beavers put on a surge and won, 78–73.

The final game of the tournament turned out to be a rematch between Bradley and City College. Bradley coach Ford Anderson predicted that his team would win easily because they intended to play a zone defense, which had been tried with some success by Ohio State.

But City College was determined to go all the way. They had trouble at the foul line, hitting only 19 of 35 free throws the entire game, but Ed Roman more than made up for the missed free throws by scoring 12 points in the first 12 minutes of play. In the first half City led by as much as 11 points.

Discouraged by the failure of the zone defense, Bradley switched over to a man-to-man defense—and it almost worked. The Braves stayed close to City all the way as both teams battled furiously.

With less than a minute to play, it appeared that City was home free with a 69–63 lead. But the fired-up Bradley squad came roaring back. In 25 seconds they scored five points, and CCNY's lead was down to one. Then, with 20 seconds left, Bradley got the ball on a bad pass. The crowd was on its feet now, screaming and cheering. Bradley's Gene Melchiorre got the ball and drove to the basket. As he jumped to shoot, City's Dambrot went up with him and blocked the shot. Dambrot came down with the ball and fired a long pass to Norm Mager, standing under his own basket. With 10 seconds left, Mager stuffed the ball in. The clock ran out and City College had won, 71–68!

Never before had a team won the NIT and NCAA tournaments in the same year. And it never happened again, either—NIT champions aren't invited to the NCAA tournament anymore. Thus the 1950 team from CCNY became the only team in history to accomplish this amazing feat.

13 · Out of a Hat

In 1950 a college player named Bob Cousy was one of the top basketball stars in the nation. Cousy played for Holy Cross in Worcester, Massachusetts, just a few miles away from Boston. At that same time Red Auerbach was the coach of the Boston Celtics. Both Cousy and Auerbach were very popular with Boston fans, and it seemed logical that Cousy would be Boston's number 1 draft choice. The Celtics were a losing team, and Cousy was a winning player. Fans would jam Boston Garden to watch him bring victory to the Celtics.

However, Auerbach didn't want Cousy on his team. The fans and sportswriters were astonished. Auerbach said the 6-foot-1 Holy Cross star was too small—pro basketball was a game for big men. He also said Cousy was "too flashy" to play Boston's kind of game.

Bob Cousy sinks a basket for Holy Cross against New York University's Jerry Remer in 1949.

He dribbled with his right and left hand, he dribbled behind his back, and he passed from every angle. Maybe that was all right for college ball, but Auerbach didn't think that was right for the pros.

Cousy didn't try to hide his disappointment. He had wanted to play for the Celtics. But he was also determined to play pro basketball. If Boston didn't want him, undoubtedly some other NBA team did. Cousy became the first draft choice of the NBA team in the Tri-Cities (Moline and Rock Island, Illinois, and Davenport, Iowa).

Then, before Cousy could play a single game, one of the NBA clubs, the Chicago Stags, went broke, setting off the weirdest shuffling of players ever seen in any pro sport.

When the Stags folded, their players were made available to other teams. Frankie Brian, a very good player with the Stags, was very popular in the Midwest, and he wanted to stay there. So he asked Tri-Cities owner Ben Kerner for a job. Kerner wanted him, but Brian couldn't just sign with the team of his own choice. Other teams in the East also wanted him, and they had the right to a chance at getting him. However, since Brian wanted so desperately to stay in the Midwest, and since he had found a willing club owner, NBA president Maurice Podoloff decided to let Brian go to the Tri-Cities—provided they gave up their number 1 college draft pick.

So Cousy was up for grabs. But he still didn't know which team he would be playing with. Two other good players were also in the "player pool": Max Zaslofsky, an outstanding shooter, and Andy Phillip, a great ball-handler and playmaker. Three Eastern teams were to choose between the players: Boston, New York, and Philadelphia. And all three teams wanted Zaslofsky.

League president Podoloff couldn't decide which player should go to which team. Each team argued loud and long for Zaslofsky. Finally Podoloff grew weary of the debate.

"Look," he snapped, "I'm going to write down the names of the players on slips of paper and stick them into a hat. The name you draw is the man you get. And that's final!"

Ned Irish, owner of the New York Knicks, drew first and came up with Max Zaslofsky. Walter Brown, owner of the Celtics, drew second and plucked Bob Cousy's name out of the hat. Philadelphia got Andy Phillip.

Cousy was elated, for now he had the chance to play with the Celtics. Auerbach was less enthusiastic. He said, "Bob Cousy will have to make the team, just like anyone else."

For a time it appeared that Red Auerbach's evaluation of Cousy was correct. Every so often Cousy's fancy dribbling and passing went awry. The tricky stuff had endeared him to college fans, but in the pros it wasn't always a good idea. In one game Cousy flipped a razzle-dazzle pass to teammate "Easy Ed" Macauley, but the ball was off target and hit Macauley on the neck.

Little by little Cousy changed his style. The "cute" stuff was used less and less, and Cousy found out he didn't need it—his natural talent was enough.

When Cousy was in the lineup, Boston had a mighty machine. Auerbach added some magnificent players to the team, such as Bill Russell, "Sad Sam" Jones, "Fireman" Frank Ramsey, and Tommy Heinsohn. This strong Celtic team reeled off one championship after another.

But the heart of the team, the playmaker, the feeder, was Bob Cousy. After a while all the good backcourt men coming into the NBA were compared with him. A coach signing a new college star would boast, "My new boy is as good as Cousy."

Finally Red Auerbach had enough of such comparisons. One night he listened to a rival coach boast about one of his players. Auerbach responded immediately and forcefully. "I'm getting tired of hearing that," Red declared. "There's *nobody* as good as Cousy— and there never was!"

That was great praise indeed from a coach who would take Cousy only after his name was picked out of a hat!

14 · The World's Greatest Shooter

As the students filed into the gymnasium, they saw a slender man in a strange uniform standing on the basketball court. He looked about 60 years old. His gray hair was cropped in a crew cut, and his black shoes were well-worn. There were strips of tape over his knees instead of the regular basketball pads. He wore a pair of maroon shorts and a gold shirt, and on the front of the shirt was his name: WILFRED HETZEL. Across the back of the shirt were the words FREAK SHOT SPECIALIST.

None of the students had ever heard of Wilfred Hetzel. He didn't look like much of a basketball player, and people were wondering if this was some kind of joke. What was he going to do? The young people were soon amazed to find out that this man could sink baskets from almost anywhere on the court.

Hetzel shot and hit from the foul line and from the side. He dropped the ball through the hoop while sitting down, on one knee, on both knees. He sank baskets with his eyes shut. He sank them facing the other way. He stood behind the backboard and arched the ball over the board and into the hoop. He even sent a dropkick through the net.

Hetzel's performance was fantastic, and the students wondered why he wasn't better known. Surely a man who could shoot so accurately would have played basketball in his younger days—maybe even professionally. But the truth was he couldn't. The only thing Wilfred Hetzel could do on a basketball court was shoot. He couldn't pass, he couldn't catch well, and he couldn't dribble.

In 1924, when Hetzel was 12 years old, he nailed a barrel hoop to the woodshed at his home in Melrose, Minnesota. Since he didn't always have a basketball, Hetzel used whatever else was handy for shooting. Sometimes he used a soccer ball, wadded-up rags, a softball, or a football. Even the weather couldn't stop him. He would practice in the heat or cold, in rain or sunshine.

All he did, however, was shoot. He couldn't very well bounce a bundle of rags or a football, so he never learned to dribble. And since he was alone, he couldn't practice passing.

In high school Hetzel managed to make the team, but only as a substitute. He seldom got into the game, and when he did his teammates wouldn't pass to him, even when he was wide open. And when he did get the ball, which was rare, he didn't shoot.

So Hetzel continued his lonely practice at home and in the school gym whenever possible. Pretty soon he could hit 98 out of 100 from the foul line. Eager to show his classmates, Hetzel gave a foul-shooting exhibition during school lunch hour. The students looked and shrugged. Hetzel was a good shooter in practice, but so what? In a game he was a bust.

After graduation Hetzel moved to Sauk Center, Minnesota, and got a job as a sportswriter. He continued practicing free throws, sometimes alone and sometimes with people watching. On one occasion he sank 467 out of 500 shots from the foul line.

But Hetzel was getting tired of just shooting free throws, so he began to fool around with trick shots. He tried shooting with his eyes closed, and after a while he could make about 75 percent of his attempts.

His reputation as a great shooter grew, and he talked some people into paying him to give a demonstration between halves of a game. But his success was short-lived, for then the Great Depression of the 1930s arrived, and nobody could afford to pay Hetzel as an "extra added attraction."

Still he continued to practice, and once in a great while the lonely sharpshooter was paid to demonstrate his extraordinary skill. This didn't discourage Hetzel, for his trick shots improved all the time. By the early 1940s Wilfred Hetzel was undoubtedly the best basketball shooter in the world. And although he didn't get many jobs, he did get more money per exhibition—about $25 per show.

Hetzel would hitchhike from place to place to put on his exhibitions. Sometimes he had to struggle through snow or huddle in the rain waiting for a lift to another town. It was a harsh, grueling life, and Hetzel's health began to fail. Only years later did he realize he had gotten tuberculosis.

Finally the effort became just too much. Hetzel could no longer sink the long 70-foot throws—or even those from 30 or 40 feet out.

He got a job as a civilian typist for the Marine Corps, giving exhibitions only when he had free time.

In 1968 Hetzel had an operation to cure his tuberculosis, and he recovered sufficiently to give limited exhibitions. Although the flashy shots were gone, he could still manage enough free throws and fancy tosses to keep an audience interested.

In 1970 a national sports magazine did a story on Wilfred Hetzel. In the article Hetzel said he had practiced about 30,000 hours and taken countless shots at the basket.

"I guess," he said with a slight smile, "I have probably shot more goals than any man in history."

He was probably the greatest basketball shooter ever, but strangely enough he was a dud in a real game!

15 · Second Fiddle

Athletes who play for teams in the New York City area have one great advantage over players in other areas—they receive far more publicity. Because many national magazines and television networks originate in New York, people in the Midwest, the South, and the West seem to get more information about New York area players than about sports figures in other cities.

When Willie Mays was playing for the New York Giants, baseball fans all over the country heard about his accomplishments all the time. But when the Giants moved to San Francisco, Mays seemed to be mentioned less often—even though he was at the height of his career.

A similar situation involved two of the best college basketball players in America in 1964–1965. One was Bill Bradley of Princeton University (New Jersey), and the other was Cazzie Russell of the University of Michigan. Both were forwards, both were high scorers, and both were All-Americans. Of course, Russell wasn't exactly unknown, but national magazines and sports programs seemed to concentrate on Bradley.

Bill Bradley deserved every mention he received. He was a great passer, ball-handler, and shooter. And he was a great inspiration to his team, which was not usually classed with the top teams in college ball.

But Cazzie Russell was spectacular too. Sportswriters who followed him marveled at his come-from-behind heroics. He saved many games for Michigan in the last few minutes with spectacular plays. What would happen if Bradley and Russell ever faced each other in a game?

Princeton and Michigan had been invited to the Holiday Festival Tournament in New York City in December 1964. After Michigan defeated Manhattan and Princeton eliminated Syracuse, the teams faced each other.

Princeton seemed comfortably ahead, 76–63, with just a little more than four minutes to play when Bradley fouled out. He

---

Bill Bradley dribbles the ball in a 1970 playoff game against the Baltimore Bullets.

had scored 41 points, about twice as many as Russell. Then the Michigan Wolverines staged a comeback. They outscored Princeton completely and dominated the backboards. Russell was picking off many of the rebounds. Princeton's lead was cut down to two, and then Cazzie tied the score with a layup. With only three seconds left, Cazzie scored the winning points as Bradley watched helplessly from the bench. The final score was 80–78. Russell had 27 points.

That didn't settle matters, however, for Princeton and Michigan—and Bradley and Russell—met again in the NCAA semifinals.

This game wasn't as close. Again Michigan triumphed, 93–76. Bradley fouled out about five minutes before the end, having scored 29 points. Russell had only 20 at that time, but he added eight more important points later to ensure the victory.

When it was all over, experts and sportswriters compared the two players. Each had some admirers. Some favored Bradley while others said that Russell had better moves. However, everyone thought it was too bad that Bradley and Russell weren't on the same team. Such a pair of forwards could give even pro teams a hard time.

Russell still had a year of college left after 1965. Bradley was graduated but didn't turn pro right away. He had been chosen as a Rhodes Scholar and left for England to study at Oxford University.

After Russell was graduated, he was drafted by the New York Knicks. He looked pretty good in pro ball, and with some experience he seemed certain to become one of the best in the league. When he was on a hot streak, no one could stop him.

Then Bill Bradley returned from England and decided to play pro basketball. Which team signed him? The Knicks. Now Bradley and Russell, two fierce competitors, were on the same team.

But the two big men seldom played on the same starting five. The Knicks had other, more experienced forwards, so only one of the two—Bradley or Russell—could play. They were competing again. Bradley finally became the starter and Cazzie became the "sixth man," the team's top substitute. Cazzie saw lots of action, and he was one of the key men when the Knicks drove to the championship in 1970. But he still spent time on the bench and again he seemed to be playing second fiddle to Bradley.

Before the start of the 1971–1972 season, Russell was traded to Golden State. There he was a starter from the beginning, scoring for a high average and leading the team. He proved he was as good as Bradley; some claimed that in many ways he was even better. When the Knicks played San Francisco, the two forwards played head-to-head again.

Playing for the Golden State Warriors, Cazzie Russell scores his five-thousandth NBA career point in November 1971.

16·Winning Streaks

All sports boast teams that have put together long strings of victories. In hockey the Boston Bruins won 14 games in a row during the 1929–1930 season. Football's Chicago Bears played 24 games without tasting defeat from 1941 to 1943 although their record was broken by one tie game.

Basketball has also had its share of winning streaks, and the story of these streaks is filled with strange coincidences. In 1959 the Boston Celtics set a new NBA record, winning 17 in a row. The Celts were finally stopped by the Cincinnati Royals in game number 18.

During the 1969–1970 season the New York Knicks challenged the old record. On October 23, 1969, they knocked off the Detroit Pistons, 112–109, and 16 games later a victory over Atlanta tied them with Boston at 17 in a row. Then the coincidences began. The next club New York faced was Cincinnati, the team that had stopped the Celtics.

Cincinnati's player-coach, Bob Cousy, had been a member of the Celtics when they set the record in 1959. Cousy was determined to keep the Knicks from breaking his old team's record.

The game was nearly over, and it seemed that his Royals would be the ones to stop the Knicks. The Knicks were trailing, 105–100, with only 16 seconds left to play. Then New York's Willis Reed was fouled. He had two shots, and he sank them both. That made the score 105–102.

The Royals had the ball now and all they had to do was hold on to it till time ran out. Cousy himself took the ball out of bounds. He threw it to Tom Van Arsdale, but New York's Dave DeBusschere dived at the ball and intercepted it. He drove to the basket and scored with a layup. Now only a single point separated the teams.

As the Royals took the ball out of bounds again, the Knicks pressed desperately. Van Arsdale got the ball, but Reed would not let him keep it. The big Knick center batted the ball out of Van Arsdale's hands and Walt Frazier recovered it. He drove in and shot as the buzzer sounded. But he missed. It seemed for a moment that the Royals had stopped the winning streak.

But Frazier had been fouled by Van Arsdale while shooting. He got two shots at the free-throw line, and he netted them both. The Knicks won, 106–105, and established a new record of 18 straight wins.

New York played their next game against Detroit—and lost. But it was only fitting. By coincidence, New York had started its winning streak against those same Detroit Pistons.

Only a year later, in 1970–1971, Milwaukee made a run for the record. The Bucks sputtered at first, winning nine in a row, and then were stopped by the New York Knicks. But the Bucks picked themselves up and went back to work on another string. This time they put together 16 consecutive victories. But once again they met New York and were beaten, falling short of the record.

The Bucks were a spectacular team, however. Again they piled up one victory on top of another until they had 17 in a row. But now there was no New York team to stand in their way. Milwaukee played the weak Buf-

---

Knick center Willis Reed scores against the Cincinnati Royals to keep the Knicks' 1969 winning streak alive.

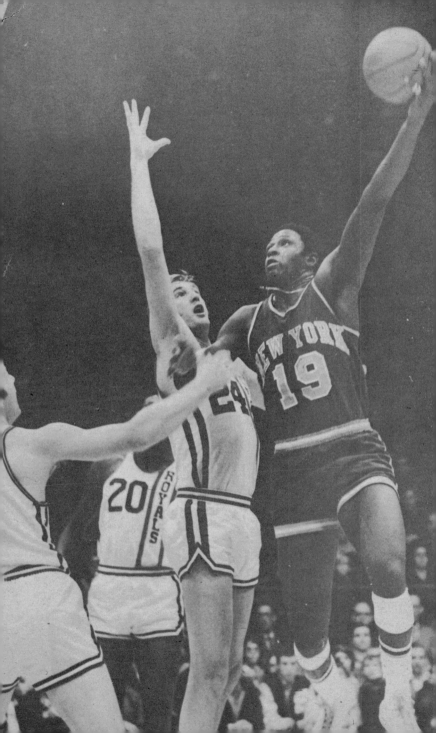

falo club and won to tie the Knicks' record of 18.

In another coincidence the Bucks then played Detroit, the team that had stopped the Knicks after 18 victories. Could they beat the Pistons as the Knicks had beaten the Royals? They could indeed—with a handy 108–95 win. The Bucks then ran their string to 20 before finally losing.

Most fans thought Milwaukee's record would stand for many years. But in 1971–1972 the Los Angeles Lakers began another victory string with a win over Baltimore. Then they bowled over one team after another. They beat an easy opponent, Phoenix, for their twentieth victory in a row and tied Milwaukee's record. Then they established the new mark with a win over Atlanta.

The Lakers rolled on and on. On December 21, 1971, they beat Buffalo and tied the consecutive-victory record for all professional sports, 26 games, set by the New York baseball Giants in 1916. Their next game was against Baltimore. The Lakers had started their streak against the Bullets, and Los Angeles won again. Now they were the winningest team in the history of pro sports!

The Bucks' Kareem Abdul-Jabbar prepares to shoot over Laker Wilt Chamberlain in 1970.

But they didn't stop there. They extended their winning streak to 33 before they lost. Who finally stopped them? The Milwaukee Bucks, whose record the Lakers had broken! The coincidences in those winning streaks seem to fit together like pieces in a crazy jig-saw puzzle.

Bob Cousy and his Celtics piled up 17 wins in a row before being stopped by Cincinnati.

The Knicks beat the Celtics' record by defeating Bob Cousy's Cincinnati team. Then the Knicks were stopped by Detroit, against whom they had started their streak.

Milwaukee started two winning streaks but was stopped twice by the Knicks. When they did establish their record, they beat Detroit, the team that had finally stopped the Knicks.

Then the Lakers toppled the old record and set a new one. They were halted at last by Milwaukee, the team whose mark they had broken.

One more oddity was that the 1971 Lakers were coached by Bill Sharman, who had played with the 1959 Celtics when they set their 17 consecutive-victories record. In a way, that tied all these strange coincidences together—but it didn't explain them. What could?

17·The Harlem Globetrotter Story

In 1906 a Jewish family named Saperstein left its home in London, England, to come to the United States. The Sapersteins settled in Chicago's Irish-German section, hoping to improve their lot in the "land of opportunity."

Their neighborhood was tough, and little Abe Saperstein, six years old, had to learn how to fight soon after he arrived. But learn he did. He often sneaked into a nearby gymnasium to practice on a punching bag. Abe also was befriended by a strapping youngster named Tom Gallery, whose father was a police captain. Tom made it clear that anyone fighting Abe had to take him on too. Before long Abe didn't have to worry about fighting. Instead, he turned his attention to other things, especially sports.

At Lake View High School Abe was a good basketball and baseball player and quite a sprinter. His basketball ability was most surprising, since he was only slightly over five feet tall and weighed about 110 pounds.

Abe went to college but only for one year. His father was a tailor, and business wasn't good enough to send a son to college for four years. Abe couldn't make enough money to work his way through. So he took a job as athletic instructor in the Chicago playgrounds.

One of Abe's pet projects was coaching a team of young basketball players called the Chicago Reds. The Reds became a winning team, and Abe's coaching success was noticed by a man named Walter Ball. Ball owned an all-black basketball team, and he offered Abe the coaching job. Abe accepted.

Ball's team played local teams in small Midwestern towns, but it didn't make much money. The team was often cheated, and there were numerous arguments. The players felt they were being treated unfairly, and eventually the club broke up.

Abe Saperstein was jobless, but he refused to admit that his all-black team was a failure. The players were just too good, too hard-working, to go down the drain. He asked the men if they would stick with him, and three of them agreed: Walter "Toots" Wright, Byron "Fats" Long, and Willis "Kid" Oliver. Then he added two more outstanding black players, Andy Washington and Bill Tupelo, to the team, and he called them the Harlem Globetrotters.

"Where'd you get that name?" asked one player. "We're not from Harlem—that's in New York. And we don't trot around the world."

Abe replied, "I'm using the word Harlem to let folks know in advance that the team is black. And I like Globetrotters because it might make people *think* we've been around."

And so, in 1926, the Harlem Globetrotters began their historic first tour. They traveled in a beat-up Model-T Ford that Abe had bought from a funeral parlor.

The team was not an instant success. One game drew such a small crowd and made so little money that the team could not be paid the $25 they had been promised. The whole team got only $5, just enough to buy some dinner.

Still, the Globetrotters managed to get by. They played almost constantly, sleeping in falling-down hotels, eating sandwiches and candy bars. They had little time off because there was always another town to reach after a game was over. To give his players a breather, Abe himself would suit up and let each one take a rest for a few minutes.

Despite this furious pace the Globetrotters won 71 out of the first 77 games they played. It is likely the team could have won all its games, for the small-town competition was pretty bad. A good part of the time their opponents were high-school boys and new graduates. Most had been badly coached and knew little of the game's fundamentals. Usually the Globetrotters took it easy. They didn't want to make their opponents look too bad because the hometown folks might get upset.

After a while they began to clown around a little bit during the games. They began with simple tricks, like looking in one direction and passing off in another direction. They would bounce passes through their op-

ponents'—and each other's—legs.

Abe noticed that the more they did this, the more the audiences enjoyed the games. Slowly it dawned on him that a new kind of team was in the making. The Globetrotters were not only great basketball players, but they were also great comics. And basketball was more than a sport—it was fun!

Now the team began to practice their tricks and devise new ones. They became fantastic dribblers, bouncing the ball between their legs and behind their backs. They would dribble while sitting on the floor, still keeping the ball from defensemen. They passed by bouncing the ball off their heads. Two players would keep passing the ball back and forth, while the other three sat down under the basket and played cards or pretended to fall asleep.

In a short time the Globetrotters became famous throughout the Midwest. In 1929 the team added the first of its "superclowns," Inman Jackson. By then they were carrying around all sorts of weird equipment—their bag of tricks was literally overflowing.

One favorite stunt was their ball-eating trick. They would pretend to argue with the referee and in mock anger threaten to eat the ball. The referee, who was in on the joke, told them to go ahead. So they did, to the delight of the fans. The ball was, of course, a fake—it was made of brown pumpernickel bread.

They also used a ball that took crazy bounces. Another ball, which was slipped into the game when a foul shot was taken, had strong rubber bands attached to it. The player shooting the foul shot would hold on to the rubber bands so that when he tossed the ball toward the basket, it would fly right back into his hands.

The lean and hungry days were over for the Harlem Globetrotters. Fans flocked to see them play, and the old Model-T Ford was replaced by a handsome bus. New clowns were added to the roster, including two of the most famous pranksters in Globetrotter history, "Goose" Tatum and "Meadowlark" Lemon. The Globetrotters were indeed beginning to "trot around the globe," traveling eventually to places such as Russia and Asia.

Sometimes, however, they had to prove that they were crack basketball players as

Meadowlark Lemon spins the ball on his fingertip for an appreciative Freddie Neal.

well as funny men. In the 1930s, in an exhibition at Woodfibre, British Columbia, their opponents jeered them, claiming that the Globetrotters couldn't win without their tricks.

Al "Runt" Pullins said to his teammates, "Gentlemen, let us show our opponents how we can play this game called basketball." The Trotters responded with probably the best basketball Woodfibre has ever seen. They won the game, 122–20, and that was in the days when scores were almost always low!

On another similar occasion the Globetrotters decided that only Runt Pullins would do the shooting. Pullins scored 75 points, almost doubling the other team's total.

The Globetrotters were Abe Saperstein's dream of America come true. There were many difficulties along the way for these black athletes and their Jewish immigrant coach. But their success proved that for those with courage and vision and the dedication to work hard, the United States was indeed the "land of opportunity."

18 · Stars of the Ghetto

It was really too hot to play basketball that July afternoon. Yet the players raced across the court at top speed, ignoring the heat as they dribbled quickly, executed dazzling jump shots, and fought for rebounds.

A 6-foot-8 forward got the ball and drove for the basket. Guarding him was a 7-foot-2 center. Near the foul circle the forward leaped, rising higher and higher toward the basket. The center went up in the air to block the shot. Suddenly the forward twisted in midair and stuffed the ball·through the hoop.

Several thousand fans were watching the game, and they cheered that sensational score for several minutes. These were knowledgeable fans, accustomed to seeing basketball at its best. They knew that had been an unstoppable shot.

Now the center had the ball and went in toward the basket. The forward tried desperately to stop him, but the big man uncoiled in a tremendous leap and stuffed the ball into the net with both hands. Again the crowd cheered and clapped.

The game wasn't being played in an air-conditioned arena. The players were on an asphalt playground in New York's Harlem, Manhattan's black ghetto. The fans were standing around the end lines and against the wire fences of the playground.

Yet the players weren't just fooling around. They went all out to win, just as if the NBA or ABA championship were hanging on the outcome. It was a matter of pride. Each player had to show what he could do for his team and his own reputation. Neither side used a zone defense—it was one-on-one all the way.

Not only were the spectators witnessing fantastic individual efforts, they were watching America's very best. The seven-foot center was Wilt Chamberlain, then in his second year in the NBA. The forward who beat Chamberlain was a local hero a year or two out of high school who played for no regular team at all. His name was Connie Hawkins and he was known to every ballplayer in Harlem as the Hawk. One day he too would be a professional star.

The Phoenix Suns' Connie Hawkins (left), a former Rucker Tournament player, guards a driving Jim Fox of the Cincinnati Royals.

Chamberlain and Hawkins were at last matched up in a Rucker Tournament game. In 1946 a young Harlem teacher named Holcombe Rucker was looking for a way to keep ghetto youngsters off the hot city streets and out of trouble in the summer. His answer was basketball.

Rucker began with four teams and one referee. Local newspapers gave his project publicity, and as the years passed more people got involved. Soon leagues were organized, with divisions ranging from junior high school through professional. Residents of Harlem, who took basketball seriously, flocked to see the games. The Rucker Tournament—really a summer league—was a huge success.

Holcombe Rucker died of cancer in 1955 when he was only 38 years old. But a former Harlem player named Bob McCullough and a pro named Freddie Crawford, who played with the Milwaukee Bucks, carried on the tournament.

The Rucker Tournament was the best-known of many organizations in Harlem and other ghetto neighborhoods that gave youngsters a chance to compete. In city neighborhoods, where there is no room for football fields and where baseball must often be played in the streets, basketball is the year-round sport.

For a young basketball player in Harlem, establishing a reputation in the parks or playgrounds may be more important than making the high-school team. Players learn fast against stiff competition from older and bigger players. They must prove themselves by going against an opponent one-on-one, as Connie Hawkins had done against Wilt Chamberlain.

Winning against a bigger man is particularly important, and graduates of ghetto playgrounds sometimes bring this skill to other levels of competition. Pat Smith from Harlem played center for Marquette University. He was only 6-foot-3 and his eyesight was poor so that he couldn't shoot from outside. Yet he held his own against the best college centers in the country. In one spectacular performance Smith played against Kentucky's Dan Issel, who was seven inches taller, and outplayed him at both ends of the court.

Al McGuire, the coach at Marquette,

grew up in a New York neighborhood where basketball was king. In addition to Pat Smith, he recruited many other great playground players to play for Marquette. One of these was Ric Cobb.

Cobb was the 6-foot-6 center for Marquette's NIT champions in 1970. But to his pals back home he was known as the Elevator Man. He got this name because he could leap fantastically high. A friend would ask Cobb, "How high today, 'Vator Man?"

Cobb would reply, "Call it, man, I'll get there." One of the Elevator Man's best tricks was to leap up and pick a coin off the top of the backboard. But since nobody could jump high enough to put the coin there in the first place, Cobb had to do it himself!

Too many potential stars in playground competition became victims of drugs. No one will ever know what heights they might have reached, because they never had the chance to prove their talents.

There was one young man, named Artie, who would usually score 30 to 40 points in a Rucker Tournament game. But Artie was an alcoholic. When he was in his late twenties,

Pat Smith

he made a determined effort to stop drinking, but he did not succeed. One morning Artie was found lying in a hallway, dead. He had drunk himself to death.

Dexter Westbrook was one of the best shooters in the playgrounds. He went to Providence College for a time but flunked out. He went back to Harlem and continued to star in the Rucker Tournament. Then he tried out for a pro team and for a while it seemed he had made it. But then Westbrook took a physical examination, and the doctors found needle marks in his arm, evidence of his drug addiction. His pro career was finished before it began. Westbrook began to steal to support his drug habit, and finally he was arrested.

Even for those neighborhood stars who never play college or professional ball, the playground competition provides some measure of fame. Those who have followed playground ball in Harlem say the greatest star of all was a young man named Earl Manigault. Earl was only 6-foot-2, but he could jump as if he had steel springs in his legs. Earl was at least as good a shooter as Artie, and perhaps better. He was as fast and shifty as Connie Hawkins. And Earl had a few tricks he had invented. For instance, he would drive in, leap high, and while still in the air he would stuff the ball through the hoop with one hand and then catch the ball with his other hand!

Nearly everyone in Harlem knew Earl Manigault. And they loved him. Earl never boasted of his abilities, never tried to prove how good he was. Once they saw him play basketball, the people knew. Earl was warm, friendly, almost always smiling. He had leadership qualities. There is no way of knowing how far he could have gone in the pros. Some say he could have become an all-time All-Pro sooner or later.

Drugs halted Earl Manigault's basketball career. Many friends tried to get him to quit, but Earl either couldn't or wouldn't stop. As his habit became more expensive Earl began to break into stores and steal. One night he was caught and sent to prison.

In 1971, after Manigault had served his time in prison, he got a tryout with the Utah Stars in the American Basketball Association. Earl and his friends were optimistic at first, but before the season started he was cut from the team. He was in his late twenties and he had been away from the game too long.

Many of the stories of playground stars have unhappy endings. But every year new players with amazing talent are coming up in this tough basketball school. The Rucker Tournament is still part of Harlem's life during the summer, and professional stars still appear, finding the competition nearly as difficult as the NBA or the ABA. The pro stars might not have trouble with college competition, but on the hard asphalt courts in the summer sun, the playground heroes still challenge them.

ABOUT THE AUTHOR

Howard Liss has written more than sixty sports books for young people, as well as books on geography and science. He has also written adult novels and nonfiction.

Mr. Liss began his career as a comedy writer, turning out jokes for such comedians as Eddie Cantor, Al Jolson, Jimmy Durante, and others. He has written successfully for the Broadway stage and for a number of nationally syndicated comic strips. Mr. Liss makes his home in New York City.